SPIES, SECRET AGENTS AND SPOOKS OF London

First published in 2003 by Watling St Publishing
The Glen
Southrop
Lechlade
Gloucestershire
GL7 3NY

Printed in Italy

ISBN 1-904153-14-3

24681097531

Design: Maya Currell
Cover design and illustration: Mark Davis
Cartoons: Martin Angel

SPIES, SECRET AGENTS AND SPOOKS OF London

Natasha Narayan

WATLING STREET

Natasha Narayan has worked as a journalist in Albania, Bosnia and Georgia and the former Soviet Union. She was also briefly education correspondent on the *Observer*, a waitress, and a satellite TV presenter. She lives in North London with her husband, daughter and son.

This book is for Louis with love.

Contents

Introduction   7

1 Early Spies   8

2 Secret Letters and Invisible Ink   11

3 Deadlier than the Male   16

4 Spies in Stockings   21

5 Gunpowder Spies   33

6 Spies of World War One   38

7 Spycraft   44

8 The Man Who Never Was   49

9 Codes and Ciphers   60

10 Gorgeous Gadgets   63

11 Spies in the Cold   68

12 Spies of Today – and Tomorrow   83

13 Spook Slang – An A-Z of
   Spy Buzzwords   89

Introduction

The Weekly Spymaster
Classified

Wanted: Spy **Location:** It's a secret, dummy! **Salary:** Loadsamoney
Company Car: Aston Martin **Perks:** Exotic travel, beautiful women,
the latest guns, mobiles and the coolest x-ray glasses

If you fancy being a desk-jockey don't apply. But if you want a job with
lots of risk, excitement and adventure – where life and death
literally hang on your cleverness – this is for you. Send photo (only the
very dashing need apply) and details to M, Canned Fruit and Tomatoes,
PO Box 200. (Sorry we can't give you an address – it's TOP SECRET)

If you believe the movies, this is a typical spy's life. But a
London spy's work is far more likely to be described by the
advert below. See if you can decode it. Have you got what it
takes to be a real 007?

DZMGVW: Z YIZRMB KVIHLM GL DLIP OLMT SLFIH

ULI OLD KZB. NLGH LU GSV DLIP RH WFOO ZMW BLF NFHG

YV EVIB, EVIB KZGRVMG. ZKKOB YLC 200.

CLUE: Any good at saying your alphabet backwards?

patient. Apply Box 200.

very, very be must you and dull is work the of Most pay. low

for hours long work to person brainy A :Wanted ANSWER:

CHAPTER ONE

Early Spies

Spies have been about for a long, long time. When Julius Caesar became the Roman leader to beat all Roman leaders there was a bloke called Marcus Crassus (who probably wore the Roman equivalent of a dirty mac and a pair of infra-red goggles dangling round his neck) hovering around in the background. Crassus was crass by name and crass by nature. He made his millions by deceit and betrayal. His armies of spies and informers were the human steps on which the great Caesar climbed to power.

Closer to home, the Goths and Picts, Normans and Saxons might have had the odd thought about getting some background intelligence on each other, as they got stuck in with their clubs and bows. But the pioneer who got spying really organized was the first of the Tudors, King Henry VII (who ruled from 1485 to 1509).

Henry had many reasons to be paranoid. For a start he was about to found a dynasty of kings and queens and there were plenty of people around who had rival dynasties in mind.

While Henry was merely a pretender to the throne (someone who pretended that he was really king and convinced a lot of people that he actually should be) the current king Richard III's agents tried to have him seized in France. Henry had to rush from place to place to escape these agents.

It was only the fact that he had his own agents – the best was Sir Christopher Urswick, the 'Recorder of London' – that enabled Henry to stay one step ahead of his enemies. Richard was pretty nasty to Henry's pals. A Tudor spy called Will Collingbourne was executed for writing a mocking couplet that called Richard a hog. The rhyme was all the rage in the ale houses of Southwark:

> **The Cat, the Rat and Lovel the Dog,**
> **Rule all England under the Hog.**

Collingbourne's execution was really bloody. The Elizabethan writer John Stow said some years later: 'After having been hanged he was cut down immediately and his entrails were extracted and thrown into the fire and all this was so speedily done that when the executioners pulled out his heart he said, "Jesus, Jesus".'

By the time Henry VII became king he had become too paranoid to let go of his army of spies. Many of Henry's spies were actually journalists – inky-fingered hacks who made a second career from passing on titbits to the king's spymasters. These early spies were called 'intelligencers' and were much employed by the first great spymaster of England, Elizabeth's I's favourite, Sir Francis Walsingham.

CHAPTER TWO

Secret Letters and Invisible Ink

In these hi-tech days lots of espionage goes on through the Internet and hacking is big business for all sorts of spies. But in history – and still today – the post was one of the main ways spies talked to spies. Sending a letter is obviously a risky business for spies, because they can be easily intercepted by enemy counter-intelligence.

There are three main ways of opening letters and packages. For 'dry openings' you use chemicals to separate the glue. For 'steam openings' you steam open the letter (obviously) and for 'wet openings' you use water.

are you cut out to be a spy?

The Great Secret Service Letter Test

TEST: This is a secret service test to see if new recruits have the brains to be a spy. You are given a sealed letter in an envelope. Inside the letter is a sheet of paper

folded in two. You are also given two thin knitting needles. Can you take out the enemy message, read it and put it back in the envelope without betraying the fact that the envelope has been opened? (And no, you can't steam it, a kettle is not part of your equipment!)

ANSWER: Many recruits when tested with this brain teaser waste time trying to use the knitting needles to pry open the letter. Others try to slit the letter with the knitting needles. Or just give up on the needles altogether. The clever answer is to insert the needles in the space below the flap of the envelope. Then carefully twirl the paper inside around the knitting needle until you can safely ease it out of the opening in the envelope. Twirl the paper around the needle in the same way when you wish to return it to the envelope. If you have passed this test, congratulations. You are a born spy!

During World War Two special devices – based on the knitting needle principle - were invented by the secret service in London.

Another way of communicating with your agents or target is invisible ink. Invisible ink has been around for aeons.

When the Roman Emperor Claudius wanted to send messages to his spies in heathen Londinium he probably just dashed off a quick message in invisible ink.

These messages can be written in between the lines of an ordinary letter, on the back of a postcard or in a handkerchief or piece of cloth. Secret writing can even be concealed by printing a photo over it – the photo can then be removed by government agents using special chemicals.

One of the most intriguing messages written in invisible ink was found by a postal censor (a man whose job it is to snoop through enemy mail) in the gloomy winter of 1914, the year World War One started. Written in the margin of a newspaper, in invisible ink, was the mysterious words 'C has gone into the North'. It added that the sender was reporting from '201'. The newspaper was postmarked Deptford and was on its way to Amsterdam.

The spies got to work and found that the only street with a 201 in Deptford was the High Street. At the address they found a baker called Peter Hahn, who obstinately claimed he knew nothing of 'C' or his whereabouts. However in his bakery the spies found an old shoebox containing a bottle of invisible ink and the ballpoint pen necessary for writing in it.

This discovery led them to a brilliant German agent called Karl Muller (Hahn had really just been his fall-guy). In 1915 Muller was executed at the Tower of London. But our clever spymasters went on inserting the coded adverts he used in local papers to deliver information to his German spymasters – and collecting the money his handlers paid Muller.

They made about £400 for British intelligence before the Germans discovered that the information Muller was sending them was worse than useless. The Germans then promptly sacked him (without realizing that you can't sack a dead spy)!

How to Make Invisible Ink

First get into the mood. Find an old beige mac, a battered trilby and a false moustache. If you have access to a microscopic camera or spy-communications satellite all the better. Then choose your method. All sorts of household products make fantastic invisible ink. Raid your kitchen store-cupboard. (But be careful who you tell about your plans, they could be in the pay of the enemy.) Solutions made with lemon juice and a bit of water, or sugar and water will enable you to write invisible messages to your agents. Honey and water is good too, as is neat vinegar and some fruit juices. Even milk works – but it can leave tell-tale gooey marks on the paper. Experiment and you'll find the best ink.

Then you need a pen, such as an old ballpoint that has run out of ink or even a matchstick or stick to write your messages with. Dip your pen into your ink – find an unsuspicious-looking card or letter and – hey presto! – your invisible message.

When you receive your answer be careful how you read it. The secret to making invisible ink messages appear is heat. If you burn your letter by trying to read it with a candle, not only will you lose the message you might even burn your house down! Even the most unsuspicious counter-intelligence agent might twig something was up when they saw the fire brigade arriving. The best way to read your invisible ink message is by holding it up to a radiator or near a warm (but not too hot) light bulb.

Good luck! And I hope your message is a worthwhile one about spyplanes and enemy troop movements. Not just a shopping list telling you to buy potatoes for dinner.

CHAPTER THREE

Deadlier than the Male

Old-fashioned spymasters used to think women were too unreliable to make good spies. But some of the most effective and most unlikely spies in London's history have been girls – at least on the surface.

It has taken hundreds of years for our spooks to work out that women can cut it in the cloak and dagger world. It was only in 1992 that MI5 had its first female head – Stella Rimmington.

How to Make Millions by Spying

Years of living dangerously in exile on the continent made King Charles II (1630-85) very suspicious. He was reluctant to trust anybody when he came to the throne – after Oliver Cromwell's king-free republic. (Cromwell had executed Charles's dad, Charles I.)

King Charles was paranoid and had not one, not two, but three secret services, and he used them all to spy on each other. But it wasn't men who let the party-loving Charles down. It was women. He fatally let his guard down much closer to home – in fact in his bedroom.

One day a lovely 'innocent-appearing girl with dark eyes, round, velvety cheeks and soft masses of dark hair' appeared at his court. She was called Louise de Keroualle – and she was a spy for King Louis XIV of France.

Charles was enchanted with Louise. He literally couldn't take his eyes off her. His other girlfriend, Nell Gwyn, instantly hated Louise and nicknamed her 'Squinta Bella' – on account of her slight squint. Nell also called Louise the 'Weeping Willow' because she would burst into tears whenever the indulgent Charlie refused one of her demands.

And boy did she make demands. She has been called 'the highest paid spy in history'. Charles gave her lands and wealth and made her the Duchess of Dover. And French Louis doled out the doubloons too. From the two kings she had an annual allowance estimated in today's money at millions of pounds.

Louise's greatest spy coup was to tell Louis the secret clauses in the treaty that King Charles had made with the Dutch. This was to have a huge influence on the whole of England's friendships with other European countries. In fact Louise and Louis managed to make King Charles ditch the Dutch and cosy up to the Catholic French – a policy that the Catholic-hating English people loathed. Many of Charles's subjects thought he had sold them out for the sake of a French bit of fluff.

How to Wear High Heels with a Sword

On 21 May 1810 an old French lady died peacefully at her London flat. She was eighty-two years old and lived surrounded by trinkets, little gilded boxes and faded silks and satins. They were the remnants of the once-lovely Mademoiselle d'Eon's past glories.

Her English lady companion was inconsolable. But controversy was growing around the mademoiselle. Was she man, woman or neither? Doctors examined the body for four days and then announced their verdict. D'Eon was in fact a man. D'Eon's respectable English lady companion was horrified at the news and never could bring herself to accept that she had been living with a man!

D'Eon was the unlikeliest spy in London's history. A slim, delicate-featured man, he seemed to prefer wearing women's clothes. In 1762 King Louis XV of France sent him to London. D'Eon had already built up a big reputation as a spy in Russia, where he had dressed in frocks and called himself Lia!

In London d'Eon got rooms in Soho's Brewer Street and became a well-known and flamboyant figure in society. He busied himself making plans of the routes the French would take if they invaded England. The French king thought extremely highly of him as a spy and made him a chevalier (or knight).

D'Eon wanted to become ambassador to England but unfortunately he fell foul of the French king's mistress, Madame de Pompadour. The powerful Madame started a mini war against d'Eon. Meanwhile he seemed to have gone a bit bonkers and started wearing women's clothes full time. Rumours spread and bets were taken on d'Eon's sex. He turned his home into a fortress and placed explosive mines in his sitting room, bedroom and study.

Meanwhile the French, who were scared that he had bags of top-secret and very embarrassing documents, tried to drug and kidnap him. D'Eon in turn decided to blackmail the French and began releasing very secret French papers to the London press.

Somehow he survived all the attempts on his life and when the French king died he made an agreement with his successor – but only after a little bit more blackmail. The agreement paid off all extravagant d'Eon's debts and gave him plenty of money. But he had to agree to wear women's clothes for the rest of his life!

D'Eon seemed to change his mind often about wearing dresses. In 1777 he complained: 'Since leaving off my uniform and my sword I am as foolish as a fox who has lost his tail! I am trying to walk in pointed shoes with high heels but have nearly broken my neck more than once.'

But even though he was dragged down by the fussy women's clothing of the day d'Eon was still a brilliant swordsman (or should that be swordswoman?).

CHAPTER FOUR

Spies in Stockings

Queen Elizabeth I, like her grandfather Henry VII, had plenty of reasons to employ spies to keep watch on her enemies. Here are six:

1. She was a Protestant Queen. Her kingdom was absolutely brimming over with Catholics desperate to put her rival Mary, Queen of Scots on the throne. If the Catholics couldn't have Mary they'd have anyone as long as they believed that the pope was the Holy Father and they wouldn't meddle with Catholic business.

2. The last ruler before her, Bloody Mary, ruled for five years. She was Catholic. Before that was the Protestant uncrowned queen, Lady Jane Grey, who lasted just nine days before her head was lopped off. And before that was the Protestant Edward VI, who lasted six years. Lizzie wanted to be queen for a lot, lot longer. And she didn't want her head to be forcibly detached from her body.

3. She had scarcely been crowned queen before waxwork dollies of her and two of her counsellors were found in an Islington stable. The dollies were stabbed with pins. Even the sorcerers were out to get her.

4. In her long reign a lot of people pretended to be her best friend – then started plotting to seize the crown. Like her one-time favourite the Earl of Essex, whom she executed in 1601. The problem is that the average smelly, hairy Tudor man just didn't believe that a woman was really and truly cut out to be queen – however much Liz proved them wrong. About the only two men Liz really trusted were her chief advisor, Lord Cecil, and her spymaster, Sir Francis Walsingham.

5. Liz never married because she said she was 'married to England'. But there were always plenty of nobles and royals plotting to get her to say 'I do'. This is not because she was a peach – though she certainly thought herself a beauty – but because they wanted to get their hands on her kingdom.

6. The Spaniards under the dastardly King Philip II were desperate to add Britain to their empire.

Wily Walsingham – The Greatest Spy Ever?

Sir Francis looked the part of a spy. He had dark flashing eyes and long creepy fingers.

His career as a spy was mixed up from an early age with his devotion to the Protestant cause. When Bloody Mary was queen, Walsingham fled to Europe to save his own (Protestant) head from her Catholic butchers. He learnt a lot about spying from the Italians. When Elizabeth ascended the throne he quickly got in her favour and started a huge secret service that kept a watch on her enemies at home and abroad.

Good Queen Bess (or Liz if you prefer) really appreciated Walsingham's efforts – but she was stingy at doling out the doubloons and such was his devotion to her cause that he spent loads of his own money on paying off the 'intelligencers'. In the end he actually bankrupted himself.

The long fingers of Walsingham dabbled in one of the most notorious spy plots of the age. It involved Mary, Queen of Scots, Elizabeth and a host of dodgy spooks.

Message in a Barrel

Elizabeth had been fairly kind to her cousin Mary, Queen of Scots when she fled Scotland, where she had made a right hash of being queen. But Mary wasn't satisfied, she wanted to be Queen of All England and Scotland herself. She rallied lots of supporters around her because apart from being Catholic she was young and pretty.

23

One of the most devoted to Mary was a young Catholic nobleman called Anthony Babbington. Now Babbington (who perhaps should have been called Blab-bington) was not a very discreet spy. But he managed to get a group of men and money together to try and enthrone Mary.

In July 1586 Babbington wrote to Mary, whom Liz had locked up in a castle, offering her his services. He wanted to: a) free her and b) put her on the throne in the place of Liz.

His letter was sealed in a waterproof pouch and put in one of the kegs of beer that was delivered to the castle every Friday. Anthony Babbington's letter was written in secret code and the plotters thought they had hit on an amazingly clever way of getting messages to and from the imprisoned queen.

Little did the plotters know that Walsingham's men had a copy of the code and were reading all the letters! In fact government spies like Robert Poley (we'll hear more of him later) and Walsingham's brilliant code-breaker Thomas Phelippes were involved every step of the way. Some historians even believe that Walsingham virtually set the whole thing up to trap the gullible Mary.

Babbington and Mary's dimwit correspondence was pored

over by these sweaty spies – they read the beery letters before either of the plotters and probably even added some juicy extras to them, egging them on to commit more treason.

On Sunday 17 July 1586 Mary's answer to Babbington was delivered in an empty barrel of ale on the back of a brewer's cart. The message from foolish Mary answered Babbington point by point. She even wrote, 'Take heed most carefully to bring the plot to a happy end.' (Actually the end for the plotters was anything but happy.) It was enough to put the noose around her neck (or the axe). In fact one ghoulish government spook sketched three lines on the envelope – a picture of the gallows.

In September 1586 Babbington and seven others were executed in the most foul way. Each man was left to hang for a few minutes; then they were taken down and their private parts cut off; finally they were disembowelled and cut into four pieces.

Lizzie hummed and hawed over Mary's fate for nearly a year. But eventually she sent the Scottish queen to the executioner. Mary was still protesting that she was innocent. She had never, she still claimed, written the fatal letter.

Walsingham uncovered loads of plotters apart from Babbington – and employed some fairly dubious characters himself. In fact almost every Elizabethan scribbler had some kind of run-in with the great spymaster. Writing wasn't very profitable in those days – so a secret agent's salary really helped in paying for the garret.

(Some say that Will – bald bloke, nice beard – Shakespeare himself was a spook.)

One of the greatest playwrights of all time, Christopher (Kit) Marlowe, was definitely a spook. Kit first became one of Sir Francis's agents when he was a student at Cambridge University. During the 1580s he was an active agent. He was sent by Walsingham to Rheims in France. In Rheims Marlowe pretended to be a Catholic and spied on the hotbed of anti-English students at the famous school for priests funded by the Catholic leader the Duc de Guise. Later he was arrested in the Netherlands for forging money.

But in 1593 he was suddenly thrown into a barrel of dung (metaphorically, at least). His pal, the writer Thomas Kyd, was taken to the Tower charged with having a manuscript that denied that Jesus was the Son of God. He said Marlowe was an atheist (that is, a man who didn't believe in God). Unkind Kyd also claimed Marlowe had given him the manuscript. (Kyd's excuse for landing Marlowe in it was that he was tortured.) This was a very big offence and Marlowe was clapped in the Tower.

Then ten days later there was a mysterious kerfuffle in Deptford:

The Spy's Reckoning Or Murder Most Horrid

Marlowe's final and bloodiest play?

Scene: The tiny upstairs room at Eleanor Bull's respectable lodging house. The table is littered with a backgammon game, spilt beer, stewed meat. The men have been locked in the room all day, sending down occasionally for extra drink and victuals. Wednesday May 30 1593

DRAMATIS PERSONAE

KIT MARLOWE: Brilliant writer of *Doctor Faustus* and government spy

ROBERT POLEY: Walsingham's spy, nicknamed 'Pistol's Man', notorious double-dealer, spook and poisoner

INGRAM FRIZER: A known heavy

NICHOLAS SKERES: Another heavy

♣♣♣♣♣♣♣♣♣

Kit (banging on the worn table, angrily): You cannot make me leave my country, gentlemen. Not to save the blushes of any of your masters.

Poley: Come, Kit. Be reasonable. You would not want to face the terrors of the rack.

Kit: No one can rack me.

Skeres (Advancing menacingly to lay his hand on Kit's shoulder): Nay Kit, we can.

Kit: I know too much.

Poley (Lays his hand firmly on Kit's other shoulder): Knowledge is a dangerous thing. *(Suddenly Frizer comes at Kit, his dagger glittering in his hand. With a swift lunge he pokes it in above Kit's right eye. The dagger goes through his socket and enters his brain. Screaming and swearing most foully Marlowe dies. Frizer pulls out the dagger and quickly bashes himself about the neck with it as Mrs Bull comes running in and takes in the blood and guts.)*

Mrs Bull: Lord have mercy, what happened?

Frizer: We was arguing about the bill. Kit didn't want to pay his fare share and he attacked me.

Mrs Bull (Horror spreading over her face): I don't believe it. You bloody murderer. You'll swing from the gallows.

Frizer (with a smug smile): No one shall hang, Mrs Bull. *(Turning to his two companions)* I trust you will back me up, gentlemen?

Frizer was right, one month after the inquest into Marlowe's death he was granted a free pardon. We've imagined what went on in that room at Mrs Bull's lodgings. But no one really knows. There are however four main theories as to what happened.

1. Marlowe was murdered on Walsingham's orders. The writer was loudmouthed and indiscreet – he was becoming a liability.

2. Marlowe was murdered because he got in the middle of a feud between two of Liz's favourites. Marlowe's patron, the dashing explorer Sir Walter Raleigh (the high priest of fags – the one who introduced tobacco to us Brits), and the equally dashing Earl of Essex, who was Raleigh's deadly enemy.

3. Marlowe wasn't murdered at all. The whole thing was a set-up. A stranger was stabbed in that Deptford room while Kit escaped abroad. When the fuss had died down he returned to England and started writing under the quill-name William Shakespeare. (This sounds really wild, but Will's first published work, *Venus and Adonis*, was dated the September after Marlowe's death!)

4. Marlowe died as a result of a brawl over a bill (this theory is so boring no one really believes it).

The Elizabethans were nothing if not broad-minded. They enlisted magicians as well as writers, as part-time spooks.

John Dee was one of the most notorious wizards of

Elizabethan times. With his assistant – an ear-less rogue called Edward Kelly – Dee talked to angels that he saw in a crystal ball. He also,

less successfully, looked for the secret of the Philosopher's Stone – the fabled ancient way to turn base metals into gold.

As well as a wizard Dr Dee was a great scholar. He was the man who first invented the term 'British Empire', for example. He wrote lots of books such as *Monas Hieroglyphica* – a work about ciphers and their relation to magic that was so clever he was the only one who could understand it. The doctor was also a fantastic early map-maker. His travels across Europe meeting brainy scientists brought him a lot of valuable intelligence, which he conveyed back to Walsingham.

Dr Dee was a great favourite of Queen Liz I and she often visited him in his house in Greenwich. But some historians think he had the perfect cover for a spy. It's just that no one suspected him of being a spook because he was such a notorious sorcerer.

Astrology was used by the secret service in 1588 when Dee passed on his calculations that violent storms were ahead . His correct reports helped Queen Elizabeth defeat Philip of Spain's attempt to invade England with his Armada of warships. (Perhaps someone should call Dee in to help the BBC's weather forecasters.)

Another time Dee sent Walsingham a message that an angel called Madimi had given him. She'd told him that a small party of Frenchmen, acting for the Spanish, were on their way to the Forest of Dean where they would bribe foresters to burn down the trees. This was being done because the Spanish knew the English were planning to build new and better ships and wanted to destroy all the timber. Government agents hurried to the forest and caught the French in the act.

Doctor Dee's heavenly message foiled the whole dastardly plot!

CHAPTER FIVE

Gunpowder Spies

Gunpowder, Treason and Plot

Remember, remember the fifth of November
Gunpowder, Treason and Plot.
I see no reason why Gunpowder Treason
Should ever be forgot.

Midnight. Bang, bang, bang. Heavy clubs thundered on the stout oak door. Deep in the vault below the Houses of Parliament, John Johnson, a swarthy, weatherbeaten ex-soldier, covered a barrel with some coal. Walking across to the door he thanked his lucky stars he had drawn the iron bolts.

'Who's there?' he shouted.

'Open up in the name of the king,' came the reply.

His palms greasing with sweat, Johnson pulled back the bolts. Soldiers in red coats filled the narrow corridors. They were led by the Earl of Suffolk.

With a grim smile, Suffolk laid his hand on Johnson's arm.

'The game's up,' he said quietly.

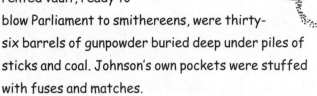

It's ye fair cop!

Equally quietly Johnson agreed to go with the soldiers. He had no choice. Hidden in the rented vault, ready to blow Parliament to smithereens, were thirty-six barrels of gunpowder buried deep under piles of sticks and coal. Johnson's own pockets were stuffed with fuses and matches.

Johnson was taken to the Tower of London. At first he was no blabber. But under the manacles and the rack he was soon screaming out his secrets. He was really, he confessed, Guy (or Guido) Fawkes.

Fawkes led investigators deep into a web of conspiracy. He was one of thirteen Catholic plotters who had aimed to blow up king and Parliament with a big bang when it opened on 5 November. The king would die along with many innocents.

The background to the plot was religion (that old turnip!). When King James I had come to the throne in 1603 the plotters had hoped he would be softer on

Catholics but he proved to be as unfriendly as
Queen Elizabeth and ordered all Catholic priests out
of the country.

So in 1605 the plotters acted. First they had tried to dig
a tunnel into Parliament. When that was too much like hard
work for posh gents, one of them, Thomas Percy, rented a
cellar right under the Parliament buildings.

The plot was soon unravelled. All thirteen of the
conspirators were caught and all were either killed as they
were captured or executed. (Except one, a man called
Francis Tresham, who is said to have died mysteriously while
locked in the Tower. Some say he was poisoned.)

But questions remained unanswered. Was Sir Robert Cecil
- the hunchback who was Sir Robert Walsingham's successor
as spymaster - the puppet master and the plotters merely
his gullible puppets? Did he in fact set the whole thing up to
warn King James I of the Catholic threat? Were some of
the plotters like Fawkes and Tresham actually double agents
who stirred the whole nasty brew?

These questions have never been properly answered.

A Forged Letter?

The government learnt of the plot on 26 October when a moderate Catholic called Lord Monteagle received a letter in his house in Hoxton. The letter, which he had his servant read out to him, began:

My Lord, out of the love I bear to some of your friends, I have care for your preservation. Therefore I would advise you, as you tender your life, to devise some excuse to shift of your attendance of this Parliament, for God and man hath concurred to punish the wickedness of this time … I say they shall receive a terrible blow, the Parliament, and yet they shall not see who hurts them … The danger is past as soon as you have burnt the letter: and I hope God will give you the grace to make good use of it.

Is the Monteagle letter suspected as a forgery because:

A) It was written in modern English, which was not possible in the seventeenth century

B) It was unsigned

C) It was very vague in content

D) No details were given of the attack on Parliament –
but the government knew where to find Guy Fawkes and
the gunpowder

ANSWER: B, C and D. (This extract from the letter is
written in modern English to make it easier for you to
understand, obviously!) Some historians think Cecil's spies
forged the whole letter to make clear how they knew about
the plot when they were pulling strings from the beginning.

The questions surrounding the whole dodgy affair are:

How did the plotters get hold of thirty-six barrels
of gunpowder when the government kept a tight reign
on supplies?

Why had no one noticed mysterious men loading barrels
across London and into the cellars of Parliament?

But there are always answers. Maybe the plotters got the
gunpowder from the black market and moved it bit by bit.
Who knows? But bear this in mind: the next time you hoist
your Guy on the fire, you just might be burning a government
double agent!

CHAPTER SIX

Spies of World War One

In the lead up to World War One (1914-18) Britain went spy mad. Anyone who was German was suspected of spookery. Newspapers, such as the *Daily Mail*, printed sensational stories about the hundreds of German spies flooding into the country.

Much – but not all – of this was a bit silly.

There wasn't much of a secret service in England at the time and the spy-catchers were often gentlemen amateurs. The actual Secret Intelligence Service (SIS) was only started in 1911. This is the forerunner of our own MI5 and MI6. (Get used to all these letters. Spooks love acronyms – CIA, FBI, KGB etc.)

Spy Kids?

During World War Two Heidrich Himmler, head of the Nazi party's secret police, seriously believed that a popular British club was a branch of MI5. Was this?

A) The Brownies

B) The Boy Scouts

C) The Cubs

D) The Women's Institute

Baden-Powell (1857-1941) was in the spook game for the fun of it. He loved dressing up and playing practical jokes. Once when he was asked to get the low-down on guns in a Balkans fortress (the Balkans is a region in Eastern Europe) he went as an amateur naturalist. In the details of the butterfly's wings he sketched outlines of the fortifications and guns. A drawing of a leaf was made to show trench lines.

On another occasion, in a reconnaissance mission of a German fort, Baden-Powell pretended to be a drunk. He soaked his clothes with brandy and staggered around helplessly. The Germans arrested him – but let him go quickly because they figured he was too sozzled to find out any secrets.

Before the war London was flooded with spies turned out by a German spy school. The school was run by a ferocious tartar, a Dr Elsbeth Schragmuller. With a Germanic passion for discipline Schragmuller believed that spies could learn a set of rules for every occasion. This is far from true and most of her spies were hopeless. They were soon caught.

This was mostly down to the work of Major-General Sir Vernon Kell, the first head of MI5. Kell had been beavering away for years – practically a lone voice in the wilderness. This was far from the glamourous world you see in spy films. When Kell asked for a clerk he was told to keep expenses down.

But Kell gradually won his battle to expand MI5. In 1910 Kell's spies were keeping a routine eye on the head of German naval intelligence, who was in London with his leader, the Kaiser. They saw him hail a cab and drive to an address in the Caledonian Road, North London, which was a dingy barber's shop. When they investigated they found that it belonged to a man of German origin called Gustav Ernst. It turned out that Ernst was acting as the post office for the Germans in Britain. He would receive packages and letters to send on to all their spies. (He was paid £1 a month for this.)

This success led Kell to gather intelligence on the German spy network. When war was declared on 4 August 1914 MI5 swooped. In a single day they rounded up twenty-two of the Kaiser's 'sleeper spies' – shattering the German spy machine. His officers were too scared to tell the Kaiser about this blow. When he did hear the news he was so furious he yelled, 'Am I surrounded by idiots?'

The Postal Clerk

But the the greatest spy the Germans had, Jules Silber, was quite different. He was so good at his job no one had an inkling of his existence.

Silber was a modest sort of a man you wouldn't necessarily notice. When he came to London before World War One, posing as a Canadian, he got English friends to recommend him for a job as a postal censor. This gave him the opportunity to read lots of secret letters.

Silber was ultra cautious. He got a room in London lodgings where he would photograph secret documents. He was very careful not to let his landlady become suspicious about his frequent absences in the evenings and made sure that he left fake stubs for concerts and plays around. When he wanted to send letters to Germany he would put them in envelopes stamped 'Passed by the Censor'.

Silber's greatest coup was the discovery of 'Q ships'. He learnt of this from a letter by a girl to her friend which dropped hints about the TOP SECRET scheme that her brother was working on.

Silber went to visit the naïve girl and in the guise of warning her not to put secret stuff in her letters learnt more juicy details about the new type of secret ships. Q ships would pose as innocent merchant boats. When they were attacked by German submarines their fake decks would be removed to reveal guns!

Silber passed these facts onto the Germans. But still no one had the slightest suspicions about him. In fact when the war ended, the Director of Military Intelligence wrote to thank him for his work. We might still not know about this seemingly ordinary censor, if Silber hadn't spilt the beans in a book he wrote when he finally returned to Germany in 1925.

Our biggest single success in the war was down to Admiral 'Blinker' Hall – who set up the famous Room 40 of the Admiralty in London, which was staffed by eccentric boffins who included a writer and several professors.

The highlight of their work was the decoding of the notorious 'Zimmerman telegram' in January 1917. This was a secret message sent by the Germans to their ambassador in Mexico. It began by saying that the Germans planned to attack all ships from 1 February, including those belonging to the neutral Americans. Then it went on to say that if America entered the war on the British side, the Germans would join forces with Mexico and invade America from the south.

Up to this point the Americans had been neutral in the war and the exhausted allies badly needed help. But US President Woodrow Wilson didn't want to get involved in a war in far-away Europe (wherezzat?).

Admiral Hall cleverly saw that this telegram could change his mind. He persuaded Western Union, the company that delivered the telegram originally, to deliver another copy to the American Embassy in London. He also provided the embassy with the code to the telegram – without letting them know that the British had decoded it.

It worked. President Wilson was furious. Within a month America entered the war. And the course of history was changed! (No wonder another great military leader, Napoleon, said that one good spy was worth 20,000 soldiers.)

CHAPTER SEVEN

Spycraft

The tricks of the spy trade have come a long way. In the early days of spookery, ordinary men in shabby raincoats sat on park benches watching their targets through holes cut out in newspapers.

Spycraft these days has more to do with satellite tracking systems, electronic and laser bugging devices and Internet hacking. But some qualities the spy needs have not changed.

These are a quick brain, patience, good observation but above all Cunning and Trickery and Slyness (Yes. You've spotted it – the last three are all the same!). A bit of ruthlessness doesn't hurt either.

A spy should be aware that he/she might be bugged at all times and take precautions like putting on the radio or speaking softly outdoors. When he/she is on his way to a meeting or dead letter drop (see spook-slang, p. 90) he/she should assume that 'shadows' are on his/her trail.

It is very hard to shake a shadow but you could:

A) Dive into a department store, weave among the counters, slip out by another exit

B) Get on a tube then get off just before the doors close. If you're followed you know you have a shadow.

C) Jump on a bus then quickly get off and hail a taxi coming the opposite way.

4) Dive into a toilet and quickly slip on a disguise, such as a blonde wig and fawn macintosh.

Disguises are essential for the successful spy. You might have a supply of hair-dye, different outfits and shoes with fake heels to make you look taller. Theatrical shops sell a variety of prosthetic noses and things that you can put in your mouth to change the shape of your face.

You can even, in the last resort, access the services of a friendly plastic surgeon who can totally alter your face! (Though you might not want to do this for your country!)

If you do know you're being followed you might have to leave the country. Always have a fake passport, fake documents and a ready supply of euros or dollars to hand!

MI6's General Tradecraft Course

When MI6 officer Anthony Cairncross was a trainee spook in 1948 he was sent on a special MI6 course. It lasted eight weeks and was held in an old building in Palace Street, Westminster. The course students used to meet regularly in a pub called the Albert.

Here is a spy tradecraft exercise:

Imagine there are twenty-four students divided into six groups of four on your course - as there were in Cairncross's group.

Your group is pitted against five groups of enemy soldiers. Their officers have left a parcel in a dead drop for one of their spies to locate. You must find the parcel. And fast. If the enemy finds it first you are dead. The problem is that enemy spies are everywhere — and you don't know where the drop is.

The six groups are each given a box file — into which they can put their notes. Once the plans are in the boxes the papers are stored in a locked cupboard in spy central HQ, and you are

warned by your course instructor that the boxes
must not be touched under any circumstances.

In three paragraphs write out clearly what you
would do.

ANSWER: No, you don't capture an enemy spy and
interrogate him or shadow an enemy spook to the
dead drop.

What you do is simple. You go to HQ and give your
password to the security guard. On the pretence of
having lost your pen you go into your office. When
the coast is clear you break into the locked
cupboard and steal the enemy's plans. They will tell
you quite clearly where the dead drop is and how it
is accessed.

OK, you're behaving like a liar and a cheat. It is
certainly not good form. But spies have got to get
used to breaking the rules!

If you still need some more spook tips, the British
businessman and spy Greville Wynne gives a handy summary
of his training in his book *The Man From Moscow*. He was
drilled to always observe principles such as:

· To study the physical characteristics of people he met.

· When meeting a colleague in public always shield the
lips with a hand or glass to prevent any lip-reading
by strangers.

• When passing messages never do so at arm's length but always close to the other person.

• For a rendezvous always inspect the area beforehand, and never arrive early or late. If the contact is missing never hang about.

PS: If you're feeling really suspicious after reading this chapter why not organize a few 'tell-tales' to find out if you are under surveillance. A tell-tale can be a single dark hair – about four inches long – with gum stuck to each side. Put it across a narrow crack in your door or your chest of drawers. If it has been moved you know that your room has been searched.

Or you can carefully measure the exact distance between your pieces of furniture to see if they have been moved. Or you can spill a very fine film of talcum powder over your surfaces – it will show up fingerprints very nicely.

Don't just take my advice. The professional spy can think up loads of their own tell-tales!

CHAPTER EIGHT

The Man Who Never Was

May 1943. Huelva, on the Spanish Coast.

Pink crabs scuttled around the man's toes, taking little, experimental nips. The waves lapped at his feet. His body was bloated with seawater and his uniform sodden and dirty.

As dawn turned into day the corpse was discovered by fishermen and turned over to the police. Locals knew they had a big case on their hands and soon the Nazis' intelligence services were involved.

The corpse was of a young English naval officer, a Major Martin. On the body the Germans discovered love letters from the officer's girlfriend Pam, along with a creased photo of her and a bank statement showing that the Major was short of money. But more thrilling was the briefcase – chock-full of secret papers strapped to the corpse's wrist.

The papers detailed the Allies' plans to land in Europe – and it hinted that the landing place would be in Sardinia and Greece. This was crucial information – the Allies had already captured North Africa and were preparing to take back Europe from the Germans. The body, which probably drowned as the result of a naval accident, was a real find for the Nazis. It could help them to win the war!

It was a huge disaster for the English and other Allies. Or was it?

In fact it was an ingenious spy hoax. Major Martin never existed. The body was that of a man who had died of pneumonia. The whole operation – down to a fake obituary in *The Times* – had been planned by British Intelligence.

Apparently even Hitler himself was conned. He believed the Allies would land in Sardinia rather than Sicily, the obvious place. German troops were diverted from Sicily to Greece and Sardinia. The wily intelligence operation, dreamed up in MI5's London headquarters, saved thousands of Allied lives and again showed how important intelligence could be!

It was just one example of the imagination and trickery which helped England win the intelligence war against Nazi Germany.

But at the start of the war, in May 1939, our secret services were made to look like pretty silly by the Germans. Two spies, Captain Payne Best and Major Richard Stevens, set out on a mission to meet a top-ranking Nazi spy who allegedly wanted to come over to the Brits at Venlo on the Dutch-German border.

Such was their foolishness that they had agreed to meet this German spy even though they didn't know his name or rank or anything about him. Some spy chiefs in London hoped it might actually be the head of German Intelligence.

Instead Best and Stevens were captured and tortured and the whole of our spy network in Europe was blown in a single afternoon!

It was a terrible blow at the beginning of the worst war Europe has known. But we fought back!

Station X

The people who really provided the brains to help the Allies win the war weren't dashing spies with killer cigarette lighters, or even sailors, soldiers and airforce bombers (though they all did their bit).

Nope. They were a bunch of brainy (and often slightly loopy) boffins who worked in a hush-hush stately home called Bletchley Park in Buckinghamshire outside London. Bletchley was code-named Station X.

This bunch of mathematicians, scientists, language buffs and other brainy people were set to work to crack top-secret German messages. These messages were sent using a newly invented machine, which turned morse code into a flabbergasting scramble. It was housed in a small metal box and was called Enigma.

Enigma was so complicated – it had millions of possible settings for every letter – that the Nazis were convinced it was unbreakable.

Thankfully they were wrong.

The Bletchley boffins were helped by the fact that before the war an Enigma machine had been smuggled out of the factory that was making them by a very courageous anti-Nazi Pole. Polish intelligence had made considerable progress on cracking early Enigma codes. They handed this work over to the British just before they were invaded by the Nazis in 1939.

At Bletchley Park brilliant mathematicians like Alan Turing and Gordon Welchman got to work on Enigma. They were part of the strangest bunch that ever worked for intelligence. One observer said the atmosphere at Bletchley was more like a chaotic student common room than a military organization.

At the start of the Bletchley project only people with Oxford and Cambridge University degrees in history and arty subjects had been recruited – by a professor of history who probably thought scientists were a bit smelly!

But then someone noticed that a mathematician had been a brilliant code-breaker. So boffins like Turing and Welchman were recruited – apparently on the basis they were good at chess.

Alan Turing was a genius. Without him we wouldn't have modern computers. But he was also a bit potty. He kept his mug chained to the radiator, cycled to work wearing a gas-mask and buried all his life savings in the form of silver ingots in the woods. Sadly he couldn't find the silver when the war ended!

During the first year of war Turing and Welchman broke the back of the Enigma codes. This was a hugely difficult task because the Enigma machine was put on different settings every day. Also there were different versions of the machine for different purposes.

Soon, thanks to Bletchley, British Prime Minister Winston Churchill could read German airforce, naval and finally, in 1942, army messages without the Nazis having a clue that their secret codes were being cracked.

The Enigma story had an enigmatic postscript when one of the machines was stolen from Bletchley Park during an open day in 2000. The machine, worth £100,000, was later posted to the TV presenter Jeremy Paxman anonymously. He returned it to Bletchley!

19 September 1940. Hertfordshire.

The parachute unfurled and the German spy attached to it slowly drifted down-wind. With a clump he landed in a field. He thanked his lucky stars, he was wet and muddy but thankfully alive.

Wulf Schmidt slowly got up and unhooked his parachute. Then suddenly he realized he wasn't alone.

Converging around him were soldiers and dogs. He was taken prisoner.

What Schmidt didn't know was that his arrival had been expected. He was taken to MI5's interrogation camp 120 and to his astonishment treated very gently.

Gradually Schmidt – who thought he would find a defeated and cowed Britain – was persuaded to change sides and become a double agent. He was given the code-name Tate and began to radio false messages to Nazis. He even radioed to them asking for more dosh.

On one occasion he was told by the Germans to wait at Victoria bus station and get on a number 11 bus with a Japanese man. He was to wear a red tie and carry a newspaper and a book. He followed the instructions and collected £200 (nice work if you can get it!). He also collected cash from the British Museum and the Tate Gallery.

The Germans thought Tate was their best spy in Britain and awarded him the Iron Cross First Class – their top medal. But in fact Tate was part of a massive and amazingly cunning British scheme.

When we captured a spy we didn't necessarily execute them – but worked on them to see if they could be 'turned' into British agents. This system was called 'Double Cross' or 'XX' and was run by MI5 agent John Masterman.

Masterman estimated that there were 120 double cross agents working for the Allies in Europe and thirty-nine who worked in the UK. They had a range of wacky nicknames like

Lipstick, Peppermint, Careless and Weasel. (Weasel was a bit of a weasel and Careless, well he wasn't exactly careful!)

The Real James Bond

Dusko Popov (1912-81) was a Yugoslav spy, code-named Tricycle by the Double Cross Committee and Ivan by the Germans. (He was, along with another spy called Garbo, XX's most successful agent.) He liked fast cars and women and took amazing risks on behalf of the Allies.

The author Ian Fleming, who also did grand work for British intelligence, met Popov and is said to have based James Bond on him.

Popov was recruited by the Germans in 1940 but he passionately hated the Nazis so he offered his services to MI6. The Germans sent him to London to do some work for them but he instead took the opportunity to be trained by MI6. They soon regarded him as a top spook.

Popov formed a Yugoslav spy ring. Its agents had code-names like Gelatine, Freak, Worm and Balloon.

His greatest coup was learning from the Germans that the Japanese planned to attack Pearl Harbour in December 1941. He flew to New York to warn J Edgar Hoover, head of the American intelligence service, the FBI. But Hoover, who thought Popov had too many pretty girls hovering around him, ignored the news. Perhaps he was jealous! The attack went ahead, the Americans were caught by surprise and Hoover was left with egg splattered on his face.

Guileful Garbo

Thankfully the information provided by Juan Pujol, a Spanish former hotel manager, was better handled. Pujol was rejected by MI6 several times before he managed to get them to take him on by tricking the Nazis. He was code-named Garbo after the American film star Greta Garbo. (This wasn't because Pujol was beautiful but because he was a convincing actor.)

Garbo had a vivid imagination. While he was seemingly based in London for the Nazis, he invented lists of fake spooks, including a Welsh fascist and a censor to keep his German spymasters happy.

Garbo's trickery was responsible for bringing about a happy conclusion to the D-Day Landings. This June 1944 battle was VITAL to winning the war. The Allies were to land seven divisions on the beaches of Normandy, in France. But they were faced with fifty-nine German divisions in Nazi-occupied France.

But Garbo radioed to the rescue. On D-Day, at 1 am on 6 June Garbo told his German controllers that Allied forces were to land in Normandy. The message was too late for the Germans to do anything about it – but it further raised Garbo's stock in their eyes.

On 9 June, when the Allied troops could have still been driven back to perish in the sea, Garbo sent the most important message of the whole XX system. 'The present operation,' he radioed, 'though a large-scale assault is diversionary in character.'

When the message arrived several crack German divisions were on their way to Normandy. But then the vile Nazi dictator, Adolf Hitler, read the message and ordered the German troops to Pas de Calais – where he believed the real Allied attack was to take place. Hitler was well and truly doubled-crossed. After reading the message he awarded Garbo the Iron Cross medal, Second Class!

hOW mAny XXX's IS thAt?

British spooks could
never have known that
the double cross
system was working if
it wasn't for a
crucial source of
information. Was this?

A) They had a spy planted high up in the
Nazi Gestapo who told them it was.

B) Mata Hari, a passionate spy, had the
ear of the head of German military
intelligence.

C) They could read decoded Enigma messages
- which showed how well XX was working.

E) They had a bug planted in Adolf Hitler's
toilet.

ANSWER: C. The success of Enigma and the
success of XX backed each other up and
helped us win the intelligence war!

CHAPTER NINE

Codes and Ciphers

Ciphers and codes were invented a long time before modern necessities like flush toilets and hamburgers. In fact for almost as long as there have been organized armies, paranoid spies have written each other strange, garbled messages in code.

The Roman leader Julius Caesar had his own special code and in London during the seventeenth century King Charles II invented a cipher which he gave his own name to. Almost all the spies based in London's foreign embassies have used some kind of code or other to send secret messages back to their governments.

Basically a code is a way of sending a secret message to a person who has the key to understanding it. You can substitute letters, symbols or numbers in your code. In some codes a symbol or word can even pass on a whole message. For example ROSE might mean abandon the safe house now.

Not all codes are ciphers. A cipher (sometimes called a cryptogram) is a type of code in which numbers or letters are substituted so only those in the know can understand the message. During the World War Two it was our spies' ability to crack the brilliant German Enigma machine's cipher which gave the Allies a crucial advantage over the Nazis.

Many of the spies in this book have used clever codes. For example, the Ruislip spies, Peter and Helen Kroger, had tiny 'one time books', smaller than a credit card. These cipher books were meant to be destroyed after they'd been used to send messages to the Russians.

There are many different ways to send secret messages. In the Book Code each spy has EXACTLY the same copy of the same book and sends messages which are coded by page number. In a simple newspaper code the spy can send messages which are agreed beforehand. For example 'LOVE YOU FOREVER DOROTHY' may mean 'ABANDON THE OPERATION IMMEDIATELY'.

During the First and Second World Wars censors read the newspapers very carefully to make sure that there were no coded messages going across to the enemy. (These days they would have to listen to radio and television broadcasts as well.) One censor even did a knitting pattern from a newspaper to ensure there was no secret message disguised in the jumper!

It's not difficult to invent your own ciphers and codes. For example a deadly message can be hidden in an ordinary note if you read every sixth word. You can let the receiver of the letter know which words to read by, for example, leaving six ink blotches on the page.

But secret government spy ciphers are getting more and more complicated. Even the German Enigma ciphers are relatively simple compared to today's complex computerized ciphers. Until 1914 most codes tended to be 'substitution ciphers' – they could be broken by comparing the frequency of letters in a hidden message with the naturally occurring frequency of letters in the language which is being used – English, for example.

A computer that can carry out thousands of decoding operations per second can crack most substitution ciphers very quickly.

In the eighteenth century a French spymaster said that an unbreakable code was an impossibility. But a good code should take so long to break that by the time it is cracked it is useless to the enemy.

So today's spies concentrate on codes and ciphers that take an extra long time to crack.

CHAPTER TEN

Gorgeous Gadgets

If you drool over James Bond's gadgets – submarine cars, exploding cigars, etc. – think again.

Real spies have fantastically clever – and sometimes downright silly – hardware that would make 007's ultimate Xmas present wish list. Plus they aren't make-believe!

One of the most famous gadgets in London spy history was involved in the strange death of Georgi Markov in 1978. Markov was not a spy, he was an exile from Bulgaria who made a living denouncing the Communist regime in Bulgaria, which in turn regarded him as a pain in neck.

One day Markov returned home and suddenly collapsed with a raging temperature. The doctor who was called in thought he had bad flu! But Markov told his wife that he had horrible suspicions: 'I was waiting for a bus on Waterloo Bridge when I felt a jab in the back of my right thigh. I looked around and saw a man drop his umbrella. He said he was sorry and I got the impression he was trying to cover his face as he rushed off and hailed a taxi.'

Markov, it turned out, was killed by a pellet filled with

poison twice as deadly as cobra venom. It is called Ricin, comes from the seed of the castor-oil plant, and had been developed by the KGB. (No wonder castor-oil is so nasty tasting.) The pellet which was fired into Markov's leg was no bigger than a pin head. The jab Markov felt was like being bitten by a mosquito.

KGB spies must have thought their poison pellet umbrella was the ultimate undetectable killing machine – like something Q, the gadget inventor in the Bond films, would have been proud of. There is no doubt they would have got away with it if Markov had not been so suspicious!

Here is some hardware right up Q's street:

BUGS: Are used in all sorts of industrial and government spying. They've become so sound sensitive they can pick up conversation within a staggering range. The KGB used to make fountain pens that contained tiny microphones. The CIA had them inside wristwatches. Bugs can be hidden almost anywhere — that means anywhere — as can microtransmitters that give away an agent's location. Sensitive areas are regularly swept for bugs — by crack de-buggers.

CELLTRACKER: A £10,000 mobile phone meets laptop computer. When a target's mobile number is punched in the computer can lock into the signal. Then all the mobile phone calls from that number can be bugged.

GLASS EYE: In the First World War a British spy couriered a secret message through enemy lines in a glass eye.

LIE DETECTORS or Polygraph Machines: Used to be high on every spy-master's gadget list. They consist of four long thin pens which are attached to instruments measuring breathing, pulse rate and sweating. Trained lie detector operators can judge whether or not a spy is lying!

At least that's the theory. In practice lie detectors don't always work. During the Cold War (the communist—capitalist stand-off that followed the very hot World War Two) Russian agents were taught how to beat lie detectors by controlling their breathing and heart rate.

But some scientists think lie detectors are flawed anyway. For example you might get excited at the mention of chocolate – because you are a chocoholic. It doesn't mean that you have hidden the secret papers inside a bar of the sweet brown stuff.

In 1985 the secret service's chiefs at MI5 headquarters were flummoxed by tests that revealed that 37% of 200 MI5 agents who took the test were lying. Either there was an incredibly high enemy infiltration of our secret service or the machines just didn't always work!

LOCK-PICKS: Spys are trained to pick locks – the best can do it with a hair-pin. But if they don't want to waste time getting their hands dirty the coolest device is the electric lock-pick gun. The spy inserts one end of the gun in the lock then switches it on. This bounces the pins in the lock until they are aligned and the lock opens.

MICRODOTS: Are tiny, tiny pieces of film. They are so small that all the words on this page and the next and the next could be fitted on to a dot no bigger than this full stop. The Germans developed microdots in World War Two. They are made by taking loads of photos and reducing them each time. Microdots have been found on spies operating in London.

MICROSPYING: Spy gear is getting so small it practically needs a microscope to see it. The newest spy cameras can be fitted into a cigarette lighter or even a tie pin. Video spy cameras are getting smaller too — so you never know when your activities might be caught on candid camera! Before the invention of mobile phones spymasters made very small portable transistors. But now anyone with a mobile can be a spy — but be warned, mobile transmitter frequencies can easily be bugged themselves.

RADIO SCANNERS: These pick up both sides of a mobile phone conversation and allow spies to listen in — before the signal fades.

RECTAL TOOL KIT: More gross gadget than gorgeous one. Escape tools such as saws, cutters, a drill and a reamer are placed in a tiny capsule to be hidden up the bum in case of a full body search. If the spy is captured he has a full escape kit stashed where no one can find it!

SPRAY GUN: The Russian KGB developed a gun which let off a spray of gas. It killed people in such a way as to make it seem as if they had had a heart attack.

CHAPTER ELEVEN

Spies in the Cold

After the nasty Nazis - and their equally unpleasant allies – were smashed in 1945, what do you think happened to all the spies?

Did they pack up their radio transmitters, cipher books and stun guns and go on long beach holidays? Or maybe go into new businesses: accountancy, farming or perhaps even teaching?

No. They stayed in the second oldest profession as a new war replaced the old one. (Don't ask what the oldest profession is.)

This one was called the COLD WAR (as opposed to the old one which was very, very hot).

The Cold War was mainly between:

The Communist Russians - who had taken over much of Europe east of Berlin in Germany and imposed 'friendly' governments

and

The capitalist Americans and their allies. The hostile border dividing communists from capitalists in Europe was nicknamed 'The Iron Curtain' by Britain's famous war-time leader Winston Churchill in 1946.

Communism is a system invented by the German thinker Karl Marx in the nineteenth century. (Incidentally, he lived much of his life in London and is buried in Highgate Cemetery.) He believed that all the fruits of the workers' labour should be shared equally between all. Under communism there would be no rich or poor, no bosses and employees. Everyone would call each other 'Comrade' and take equally from the pot of wealth. Sadly in many communist countries, a dictatorship of the workers ended up becoming a dictatorship of the communist bosses. It was a bit like any dictatorship really, but as people didn't get extra pay for working extra hard, they didn't bother and there wasn't much to buy in the shops. Many people wanted to escape to capitalist countries because they had more chance of getting rich and eating big hamburgers!

The Russians took all this talk of iron curtains quite literally and built a wall dividing East Berlin from West Berlin in August 1961. Presumably they couldn't actually find enough scrap iron to make a curtain.

Most of the skulduggery went on in New York and Berlin

and Washington – but as America's Number One Ally, Britain was drawn in. As the Russians and their friends (the Bulgarians, Czechs, Poles etc) stuffed their embassies with unnecessary 'air attachés' and chauffeurs, third secretaries and cleaners, London became a hotbed of international intrigue.

House of Spooks

The milkman didn't twig there was anything odd about 45 Cranley Drive as he left his daily pint on the porch. Nor did the boy on his bike as he tossed in a rolled-up bundle of papers.

The big bungalow in suburban Ruislip, West London was owned by a nice Canadian couple, Helen and Peter Kroger. They were middle aged and quietly spoken. They didn't have rowdy parties. They got on with the neighbours. And they owned a lovely bookshop at 190 Strand in London. They were the height of suburban respectability.

But in 1960 the neighbours were in for a nasty shock as teams of secret agents led by a Superintendent Smith from Scotland Yard descended on 45 Cranley Drive. Smith asked Mrs Kroger to accompany them to the station for further questioning. She quietly agreed. It was all very polite.

But first, Mrs Kroger asked, 'Could I stoke the boiler?' 'Certainly,' replied the copper, 'but let me see what's in your bag.'

Then all hell broke loose, as Mrs Kroger refused to let go of her bag.

After a struggle the agents got hold of Mrs Kroger's bag. No wonder she didn't want to let go. Inside was a six-page letter in Russian, three microdots and a typed sheet of code.

This was only the beginning. Cranley Drive, it turned out, was a hotbed of spying hardware.

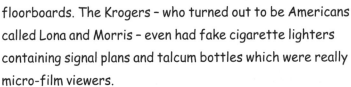

The bathroom could be converted into a darkroom, a micro-dot reader and several thousand dollars were found in a secret compartment in the attic. A radio transmitter was found in a cavity under the floorboards. The Krogers – who turned out to be Americans called Lona and Morris – even had fake cigarette lighters containing signal plans and talcum bottles which were really micro-film viewers.

The busting of the Krogers' spy nest was the end of a long road which had started with an ordinary clerk ... Harry Houghton worked at the top-secret Underwater Weapons Establishment at Portland in a very minor role.

But Houghton, who didn't earn very much money, was always hanging out at flashy hotels and drinking expensive cocktails with his girlfriend Ethel Gee. Where did he get the dosh? MI5 trailed Houghton for a year and found that he frequently met a Canadian businessman called Gordon Lonsdale.

Secret agents watched as Houghton and Lonsdale exchanged packages.

What was going on? It didn't take MI5 long to guess that it was dead dodgy.

This Gordon Lonsdale was a real character. Like James Bond he had a reputation for being a bit of a ladies' man and he entertained the girls lavishly at his swanky digs at the 'White House', Albany Street, in Central London. Lonsdale ran a company selling juke boxes and bubble gum machines, which was making a lot of money. He seemed every bit the entrepreneur, charming, rich and popular. In fact he was so popular that he had made convenient friendships with army colonels at nuclear bomber bases.

On a freezing January evening in 1961 as Houghton, Gee and Lonsdale were up to a bit of skulduggery with letters and parcels near the Old Vic Theatre in Central London, MI5 agents pounced. They picked up all three spies in one swoop.

Houghton and Gee soon spilt the beans, Houghton admitting, 'I've been a bloody fool.' But Lonsdale – a pro to his fingertips – was a harder nut to crack. He never said a word. However MI5 agents were soon on to him. His real name, it turned out, was Konon Molody, and he was a colonel in the KGB.

The Russian was a perfect example of a 'sleeper agent' – and showed just how long-term the KGB's planning was. Molody had been taken to the US by an aunt at the age of eleven. He was born within a year of the real Lonsdale, whose identity he stole. Educated in California, Molody's accent and behaviour was that of the perfect American.

He loved London and once admitted that his ambition was to 'live like an English country gentleman'. Lonsdale/Molody was sentenced to twenty-five years in prison – but he never got down in the dumps. In prison he translated three books into Russian and started writing a Chinese/Russian dictionary.

He was convinced that the KGB would do anything to get

him home and he was right. After a few years of prison he was exchanged for a British businessman, Greville Wynne, who had been convicted of spying in Moscow.

Is Anybody Around Here Not a Double Agent?

The arrest of a famous gang of spies was a big success for the secret service. It was one they badly needed. Because in the late 1950s and early 1960s more and more double agents kept tumbling out of MI6's woodwork.

Some of the secret Russian spies in MI6 and other high-up places in the government were in top jobs. The rash of communist spies who had 'penetrated' British security led our spooks to get very paranoid and start thinking EVERYONE was a spy. Both the boss of MI6 (the spooks who spy on spooks abroad) and the boss of MI5 (the spooks who spy on spooks in London and England) came under suspicion and were investigated.

Double and triple agents were everywhere. Meanwhile spies defected (i.e. escaped) from Russia to the West. These Russians kept giving more intriguing clues to yet more English 'traitors' in London. Our spooks were puzzled. They thought some of these Russian defectors might be 'fakes' who were really just pretending to reveal secrets and were in actual fact planting nonsense to waste British spies' time.

It really was all a bit confusing.

Most of our home-grown Russian spies were clever and from really good (i.e. posh) backgrounds. They went to expensive schools and a lot of them studied at Cambridge University and were good pals. Their dads went to posh schools too and had lots of plummy friends. They were 'ideological spies' – this means they did their spying for Russia because they honestly believed communism would sort out the world's problems, rather than for bundles of cash. This made them very hard to catch!

When these 'idealists' applied for a top secret job the interviews went something like this:

INTERVIEWER (Rising): Kim, old boy, lovely to see you again. How's the pater*?

KIM: Oh super, actually. He's taken up golf now that he's retired from running the country.

INTERVIEWER: Lovely, lovely. Must see if we can fit in a couple of holes** soon. So you want to be a spy, do you?

KIM: Rather. I must say I do quite fancy a bit of cloak and dagger work.

INTERVIEWER: Splendid. Can you start Monday?

KIM: What about the positive vetting?***

INTERVIEWER: Oh, we'll just send a few of our chaps round to have a chinwag with some of your pals and so on. Can't see much of problem there. Fill in the forms that Marcia gives you at the door – standard stuff. You know, just to say if you've come across any pinkos**** or anything … Well, see you Monday and say hello to your lovely little sister from me.

(Note *pater = dad **holes = rounds of golf ***positive vetting = was meant to be a very thorough process to check that the candidate for the secret service didn't have any dodgy pals/secrets. In fact with posh spies it was often over before it began. ****pinko = slang for communist)

No wonder our secret service was more leaky than a sieve. Three things made experts feel sure that the Russian KGB penetration of MI6 and MI5 went right to the top:

A) All of our double agents met horrible ends. It was

almost as if the Russians knew about them despite the fact that we were so brilliant at running 'Double Cross' – the double agent system against the Nazi Germans during World War Two.

B) No Russian KGB spies who decided they wanted to start a new life in the West ever chose England.

C) Lots of our operations went mysteriously wrong. Even when we did arrest a top KGB spy (like Lonsdale) the person who 'handled' him for the Russians often escaped – like they'd been tipped off – before we could arrest them.

So who were the dastardly double agents in our spycamp? Here is the (two-face) spook hit list:

1. DONALD MACLEAN – Was a British diplomat who knew others in the gang below at Cambridge University, where he was recruited as a Russian spy. He was gay, an alcoholic and a bit of a blabbermouth for a spook. On one occasion he abused a CIA officer's wife and made a life-long enemy. It was while he was posted in America that he got hold of top-secret atom bomb information, which he gave to the Russians. He was warned that the Americans suspected him of spying and suddenly vanished in 1951. He turned up later in Moscow, Russia, with his pal Guy Burgess.

2. GUY BURGESS – Another spy from Cambridge University! Burgess was a wild man, who liked his drink, often forgot to pay bills and was also gay. He was also a diplomat and it is believed forced his pal Maclean to scarper with him to Moscow.

3. KIM PHILBY – 'I was given the job of penetrating British intelligence and told it did not matter how long I took,' Philby declared in his autobiography. He was also recruited at Cambridge University by the Russians and amazingly actually rose to become head of MI6's Section IX. Section IX was, you've guessed it, meant to counter Russian espionage. But Philby gave the score away before our hopeless spooks even got started. Philby was so charming and clever that he was often spoken of as a future boss of MI6.

As a double agent Philby often had to think quick. Just after World War Two, for example, two Russian defectors appeared at the same time! Philby passed on one case but the other, a spy called Constantin Volkhov, could have betrayed him so he rushed to Istanbul. He must have tipped the Russians off because Volkhov was seen, heavily bandaged, being hustled by heavies into a jet bound for Moscow.

After Burgess and Maclean defected the heat was on for

Philby, especially from the Americans. He retired from the secret service and became a journalist – but he continued a bit of spookery on the side. Despite the evidence against him, it was another eleven years before he was finally called on to answer some serious questions. In January 1962 he vanished – and turned up in Moscow six months later.

4. SIR ANTHONY BLUNT – A relative of Queen Liz II's mum. Anthony Blunt was recruited by the Russians in the 1930s. He joined MI5 in 1940. During the Second World War he helped the Russians by giving them the exact dates and plans for the Normandy landings. Though he left MI5 in 1945 he kept up ties with it. Blunt became Keeper of the Queen's Pictures and got a knighthood for his work. He was a friend of the royals but after Burgess and Maclean fled to Russia in 1951, Blunt came under suspicion too and was interviewed by MI5 eleven times. He was good at keeping secrets because it was only in 1979 that he was finally publicly revealed as a Russian spy.

There were other double agents we know about. One was the MI6 spy George Blake, who was sentenced to forty-two years in prison in 1961. This represented one year for every British agent he had exposed to probable death! But sensationally Blake escaped from Wormwood Scrubs prison in London five years later – by climbing down a ladder made from knitting needles!

Perhaps there were other Russian spies we will never know about.

The Cold War came to an end in November 1989 when the people of East Berlin tore big holes in the wall separating them from the capitalist West with their bare hands. The Berlin Wall crumbled and so did the communist East German government. One by one communist countries of Eastern Europe fell like nine-pins. 1989 was a big year.

The world was lucky in that there was a visionary (a man who could see a long way into the future) leader in Russia at this time. Instead of sending in the tanks to crush the Eastern European rebellion, the Russian President Mikhail Gorbachev – known as Gorby – saw that the times, they were a-changing. By 1991 the small countries that made up the Soviet Union had left – leaving Russia, the boss, with just a fraction of its old empire.

And then even Russia had elections.

Communism – at least the Russian-backed kind – was toast. The Cold War had ended.

So did that mean the spies finally packed their surveillance gear up and moved into landscape gardening?

You've got it. The answer is a big, fat NO.

Garden Shed Spies

Think of three things you could do with your garden shed. You could keep:

A) Compost and lawnmowers and bits of old junk in it (the obvious solution);

B) All the gear that annoys your parents so much in it and make a cosy den for yourself (a much better use of space);

or

C) You could turn your garden shed into a high-tech espionage centre as two East German spies, Sonja and Reinhard Schulze, did. The Schulzes were certainly imaginative about the use to which they put the shed, in the garden of their house in the Greater London suburb of Cranford, Middlesex. Concealed in a blue plastic air freshener were three high-tech gadgets to send secret coded messages to Berlin.

The Schulzes – who were arrested as the result of a tip-off from a defector – were part of an international ring that was trying to get information about a European defence project. This was a spy satellite called Ariane. The Russians and their friends were desperate to know what Ariane could do. The Schulzes were sentenced to ten years in prison at the Old Bailey in 1986.

 CHAPTER TWELVE

Spies of Today - and Tomorrow

Baked beans, fried eggs, sausages, two slices of bread and a mug of tea. You are in the middle of a slap-up Sunday breakfast. Your sister whinges that she hates sausages, while your mum hides behind the newspaper.

So far, so normal.

WHOOSH. Hundreds and thousands of miles away BIG BROTHER is watching you. While you bicker on heedlessly, a satellite is spying on YOUR FAMILY. It can tell what you're having for breakfast and can even read Mum's newspaper.

Science fiction or fact?

100% Fact. Spy planes with infra-red imaging can even tell, from the heat shadows left behind, how many planes were on the runway hours after they have taken off.

With advances in super-hi-tech wizardry, spy satellites and snooping devices, guns and lasers are hugely complicated. The spy of today and tomorrow has at his/her fingertips more hardware than you can think up.

Much of the new cloak and dagger work is in the new communications. Much of the world now works on the Internet – but Internet records and emails can be logged and deciphered. Even the ones in secret code! And hackers can tap into computers to play around with and alter your details.

In 2001, one teenager hacked into hundreds of online stores and stole thousands of personal credit card numbers. Using one of the credit cards he sent a carton of medicines to Bill Gates, boss of Microsoft, one of the biggest computer companies in the world.

With the end of the Cold War spying has moved on. Tabloid journalists spy on celebrities to get stories for their newspapers. Companies spy on other companies to get valuable hi-tech information and secrets. And the secret service spies on another lot of terrorists who want to blow up buildings and people.

As the world becomes more hi-tech the job is actually getting easier for spies of all sorts. For a small fee those in the know can get details of any Londoner's bank account. A bit more dosh and you can buy telephone records, email records, tax details, criminal records and even secret medical records.

Spooks can have their tabs on you within a matter of hours!

Meanwhile the government can identify you by your fingerprints, the iris in your eyeball and identity cards – which have all sorts of personal codes on them.

But the new generation of 007s will be able to spy deep inside your body - not just on the outside.

DNA is the new spy battle-station. DNA is coiled up inside the trillions of cells inside us. It is the building blocks of life, the genes that determine how we look and even how we behave. Every person's DNA is even more unique to them than their fingerprints.

DNA Detectives

An enemy agent is after you. They want to know everything about your DNA. You want to stop them. From what evidence can they find your DNA?

1. Your photograph

2. A piece of discarded dental floss

3. Some gum that you have chewed

4. A piece of snot

5. Earwax on a cotton bud

6. Your computer password

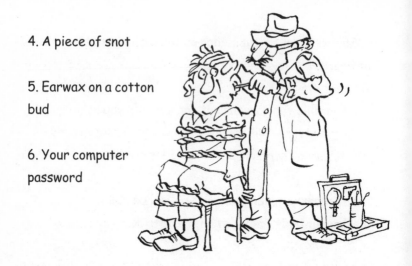

ANSWER: 2, 3, 4 and 5. DNA can be tested and traced from all sorts of discarded bits and pieces of our bodily juices (yuck). Spies and private detectives can now snoop through people's cast-out rubbish to find bits that have their DNA on them. This happened in 2002 to a millionaire Hollywood producer who was being spied on by a rival!

In labs and universities around the world scientists are working hard to trace the secrets of DNA. They can already tell an amazing amount from a bit of earwax.

For example, a spook with your earwax could predict your height, weight, hair and eye colour. They could tell where you have been – from bits of DNA you have left behind, for example from the rim of a glass you drank from in a café.

They are already beginning to tell what diseases you might develop. For example your DNA might show that you have a tendency to develop rheumatism.

In the future the DNA snoops might even be able to tell if you easily lose your cool, or if you like chicken tandoori!

Imagine the advantages that an enemy spook would have if they had the DNA of our Prime Minister – and could tell he was going to get really sick from flu when he was sixty. What a great time to start a campaign to sabotage his government.

So this is how future spook, Marla Craft, might operate.

Sitting in her laboratory aboard space station XVX Marla selects target Y, a man named Ron. Ground operatives steal a bit of Ron's discarded dental floss. Marla puts it through SpaceMind analysis and from its files finds out that Ron has two kids, is five feet ten, and will develop heart disease in ten years' time. He has a tendency to be overweight.

Marla also finds out – and all from Ron's DNA – that he can easily be provoked and that chocolate is a good thing to blackmail Ron with. His son Sam is predicted to grow up to dislike Ron.

Spy satellites are targeted on Ron and from then on his every waking moment is recorded. Sleep monitors record his dreams.

If Marla's earthling spies don't manage to track and trap Ron with information like this behind them, well bad luck. They can't be very good at their jobs.

After all, no matter how clever the spy gadgets get you can't overcome good old Human Error.

CHAPTER THIRTEEN

Spook Slang - An A-Z of Spy Buzzwords

AGENT PROVOCATEUR – A spy employed to make lots of mischief and confuse the enemy.

BLACK OPS – Secret spy operations which can include murder and kidnapping.

BLOWN – A spy whose cover (see p.90) has been compromised to the enemy. They know that he is not really a chauffeur but is head of the KGB's London section!

'C' – The initial by which the head of MI6 has been traditionally known since the organization's early days. James Bond's boss's name 'M' is cribbed from this.

CACKLEBLADDER – Spy slang for making a live body look like a dead one with plenty of ketchup or chicken blood smeared over it. A Cacklebladder op is done to confuse enemy agents.

89

CIA – Central Intelligence Agency – America's main spy network. Its nickname is 'The Company'.

COBBLER – A passport forger.

COVER – The fake life story, job etc. given to a spy to protect his real identity and work.

DEAD DROP – A secret hiding place for messages, in hollow tree trunks or under gravestones for example, which can be picked up later.

DEFECTOR – A spy who deserts his own country and escapes to another (enemy) country. Often they bring valuable secrets with them.

DIRTY TRICKS – Another name for 'black ops'.

DISINFORMATION – Smears and incorrect information given to the enemy. MI6 used disinformation a lot against Nazi Germany.

DOUBLE AGENT – A spy who secretly works for another country. Some double agents appear to work for two sides but are really loyal to one. There can be triple or quadruple agents but these are playing a dangerous game.

FIRM – The nickname for MI6.

FUMIGATING – Checking for bugs and listening equipment.

GCHQ – Government Communications Headquarters. Based in Cheltenham this government spy station listens to messages and broadcasts from all over the world. It is linked to hi-tech satellites.

IN THE FIELD – Spies at work in enemy territory.

KGB – Komitet Gosudarstvennoy Bezopasnosti – the Russian spy network.

LION TAMER – A heavy called in to do the spy's dirty work.

MEASLES – A murder victim whose death is made to look accidental has 'measles'.

MI5 – Britain's internal spy service, also called the security service.

MI6 – Britain's foreign spy network also called the secret service or SIS (the Secret Intelligence Service) and nicknamed The Firm.

ONE-TIME PADS – Tiny code books carried by undercover spies. They are meant to be destroyed after they are used.

PAVEMENT ARTISTS – A surveillance team who keep watch on a suspect.

SAFE HOUSE – A hideaway for people the government wants to protect.

SLEEPER – A spy who does not actually work for the enemy until he gets into a position to be of real use.

SOAP – Sodium Pentothal, a truth drug.

XX – The Double Cross Committee which was set up during World War Two to run double agents (loyal to the British) against the Nazi Germans.

ZOO – A police station.

So next time you pick your nose, pinch your sister's chocolate Easter egg or listen in on a phone conversation - remember, Big Brother might just be watching you.

Other books from Watling St you'll love

CRYPTS, CAVES AND TUNNELS OF LONDON
By Ian Marchant
Peel away the layers under your feet and discover the
unseen treasures of London beneath the streets.
ISBN 1-904153-04-6

GRAVE-ROBBERS, CUT-THROATS AND POISONERS OF LONDON
By Helen Smith
Dive into London's criminal past and meet some of its
thieves, murderers and villains.
ISBN 1-904153-00-3

DUNGEONS, GALLOWS AND SEVERED HEADS OF LONDON
By Travis Elborough
For spine-chilling tortures and blood-curdling punishments,
not to mention the most revolting dungeons and prisons you
can imagine.
ISBN 1-904153-03-8

THE BLACK DEATH AND OTHER PLAGUES OF LONDON
By Natasha Narayan
Read about some of the most vile and rampant diseases ever
known and how Londoners overcame them – or not!
ISBN 1-904153-01-1

GHOSTS, GHOULS AND PHANTOMS OF LONDON
By Travis Elborough
Meet some of the victims of London's bloodthirsty
monarchs, murderers, plagues, fires and famines – who've
chosen to stick around!
ISBN 1-904153-02-X

RATS, BATS, FROGS AND BOGS OF LONDON
By Chris McLaren
Find out where you can find some of the creepiest and crawliest inhabitants of London.
ISBN 1-904153-05-4

BLOODY KINGS AND KILLER QUEENS OF LONDON
By Natasha Narayan
Read about your favourite royal baddies and their gruesome punishments.
ISBN 1-904153-16-X

HIGHWAYMEN, OUTLAWS AND BANDITS OF LONDON
By Travis Elborough
Take yourself back to the days when the streets of London hummed with the hooves of highwaymen's horses and the melodic sound of 'Stand and deliver!'
ISBN 1-904153-13-5

PIRATES, SWASHBUCKLERS AND BUCCANEERS OF LONDON
By Helen Smith
Experience the pockmarked and perilous life of an average London pirate and his (or her) adventures.
ISBN 1-904153-17-8

REBELS, TRAITORS AND TURNCOATS OF LONDON
By Travis Elborough
What could you expect if you were a traitor – and you were discovered? Take your pick from some of the most hideous punishments ever invented.
ISBN 1-904153-15-1

WITCHES, WIZARDS AND WARLOCKS OF LONDON
By Natasha Narayan
Quite simply the bizarre history of London, full of superstition, magic and plain madness.
ISBN 1-904153-12-7

In case you have difficulty finding any Watling St books in your local bookshop, you can place orders directly through

BOOKPOST
Freepost
PO Box 29
Douglas
Isle of Man
IM99 1BQ

Telephone: 01624 836000

email: bookshop@enterprise.net